RESTORING
HOPE

THE JOURNEY THROUGH
GRIEVING LOSS

A Ten-Week Bible Study

Ann Rita Frazier

ISBN 978-1-63885-175-2 (Paperback)
ISBN 978-1-63885-176-9 (Digital)

Covenant Books, Inc.
11661 Hwy 707
Murrells Inlet, SC 29576
www.covenantbooks.com

Behold, children *are* a heritage from the Lᴏʀᴅ. The fruit of the womb *is* a reward. Like arrows in the hand of a warrior, so *are* the children of one's youth. Happy *is* the man who has his quiver full of them. —Psalm 127: 3–5

To my children, grandchildren, and great-grandchildren. You are the heritage and blessing from the Lord.

ACKNOWLEDGMENTS

I could not write this book without the revelation of the Holy Spirit, the love of God, and the grace of Jesus Christ. I humbly acknowledge that God is my source of inspiration, and He is the giver of all good things. Any part of this book that is good came from God, and any part that doesn't ring true can be attributed to my missed perception of what God was teaching me.

I want to thank Lee and Denise Boggs for their encouragement and support in writing this book. I used Denise Boggs' stages of grieving from her book, *Healing and Restoring the Heart* (2019) as my model to share the process in this Bible study. The principles I share about the grieving journey in this book were tested and tried in my life.

I am forever grateful for the way God used Living Waters Ministry to bring healing to my heart. Denise and Lee Boggs confirmed scriptures that I received from the Lord in my grieving journey and helped me understand the process.

This book is about my journey, but it can't be shared without mention of my daughter, son, and family. I want to thank my daughter, Molly, for loving me through the hard times and for her patience while I spent the time to record my journey in this book.

A special thank you to my son—David—and his wife, Denise. Their unconditional love is a gift that has shown God's redeeming love to me. The love and support from my family helped me through many challenges and opportunities on my journey to healing.

A special thanks to my friend and prayer partner Carolyn Thomas. She has prayed for me and listened to my many stories for seventeen years. Her help in writing and editing this book has been invaluable. I would also like to thank my editor Andrea Merrell for her help in editing the manuscript.

CONTENTS

INTRODUCTION

A storm was brewing. Whirlwinds of confusion and floods of disappointment raged against the foundations of my faith in God and His Word. The atmosphere changed, striking the core of every relationship with each strong gust of wind. This storm would be a test of where I put my trust and what I believed.

Would my faith stand strong, unshaken by the storm?

Directly after I felt the storm approaching, the winds of adversity hit. I experienced the loss of my best friend and husband, Jack. Without warning, he died suddenly at the age of fifty-three.

I knew my life would never be the same.

As I walked the grieving path after his death, I found some valuable treasures of revelation that helped me along the way. I want to share them with you.

Everyone's story of loss is different and personal. But as you seek God's help on the grieving path, you will recognize the challenges and opportunities as you move forward. I invite you to come with me down God's path in this Bible study about grief and loss.

In this ten-week study, you will find treasures in God's Word, a way to apply His truth to your life, and my testimony of the Lord's healing and restoration along my own journey. You will find each step leading you to a greater dependence and awareness of the Lord's involvement in your life.

This *Restoring Hope* Bible study opens with a loss and ends with hope for the future. In this journey, you will begin with the initial place of shock, proceed through the "valley of the shadow of death," and arrive at the heights of healing and restoration.

This study has scriptures, testimony, prayers, questions for reflection, and life application with room for responses within each chapter. This approach is an interactive way of learning and healing through meditation on God's Word by facing pointed questions to journal and pray through. Are you ready to begin?

In this study, you will be able to do the following:

- Chapter 1: Shock—identify the characteristics of shock, how it affects you, and how you react to life in the initial stages of grief.
- Chapter 2: Anger—identify who you are holding responsible for your loss.
- Chapter 3: Sadness—recognize cycles that can trap us as we try to meet the need for comfort. We look at Job's friends and their response to his losses.
- Chapter 4: Facing the Loss—identify what you have lost. We look at Nehemiah as he surveyed the broken gates of Jerusalem.
- Chapter 5: Forgiveness—forgive the person you might blame or hold responsible for your loss. We will look at forgiveness as the key to release guilt or anger held in your heart. We also look at Joseph's example of forgiveness for his brothers.

- Chapter 6: Release—release the person you have held responsible for the loss and the events surrounding it. We look at Naomi and how she released her losses and received a blessing from the Lord.
- Chapter 7: Facing the Reality of the Loss—confront the reality of every area of your life where you have experienced loss. We also look at what you have used to replace the loss.
- Chapter 8: Final Release—release expectations and disappointment and surrender to the Lord.
- Chapter 9: Acceptance—discover the peace that comes from God with surrender, accepting and embracing your new life with changes, and choosing to walk in the peace of the Lord instead of the pain.
- Chapter 10: Overcomers—understand how God redeems your losses and brings new opportunities into your life. You will use your testimony to bring the same comfort to others that God gave to you.

I encourage you to find some friends who will go through this study with you. You will discover the support of those who share your faith in the Lord and desire to walk with you down the grieving path to be part of the healing process.

If you are new to Bible studies as I was when I started my first one in 1993 (*Experiencing God: Knowing and Doing the Will of God* by Henry T. Blackaby and Claude V. King), I encourage you to allow the Spirit of God to speak to you as you go through each scripture.

Psalm 107:1–2 is my mandate from the Lord to share the scriptures that encouraged me and the testimony of what God did in my life.

> Oh, give thanks to the LORD, for He is good! For His mercy endures forever. Let the redeemed of the LORD say so, whom He has redeemed from the hand of the enemy. (Psalm 107:1–2)

If you have not asked Jesus to be your Savior and Lord, you can begin with this prayer:

> Lord Jesus, I believe You exist and that You came to save me from my sins. I repent for the things I have done that did not honor You. I receive Your forgiveness and give You my heart. Today I make You Lord of my life and give You full permission to direct my steps and lead me by the Holy Spirit to read the Bible and apply it to my life.

If you have already made a commitment to follow Jesus, ask God to give you revelation as you study His Word. Make these words from Paul's letter to the Ephesians personal:

> That the God of our Lord Jesus Christ, the Father of glory, may give to you the

spirit of wisdom and revelation in the knowledge of Him, the eyes of your understanding
being enlightened; that you may know what
is the hope of His calling, what are the riches
of the glory of His inheritance in the saints.
(Ephesians 1:16–18)

Then pray:

Father, I ask that You give me the spirit
of wisdom and revelation of insight into Your
Word and a deep intimate knowledge of You. I
ask that the eyes of my heart would be flooded
with light so I may know and understand the
hope to which You have called me and the rich-
ness of Your glorious inheritance for those who
are committed to You. In Jesus's name, amen.

CHAPTER 1

Shock

Yea, though I walk through the valley of the shadow
of death, I will fear no evil; for You are with me;
Your rod and Your staff, they comfort me.

—Psalm 23:4

The very moment I entered the traumatic event of my husband's death, my initial reaction was shock. The kind of shock that left me shattered as though a tornado touched down in my life. The impact of that event left me looking at the pieces of my life like a scattered puzzle on the floor. I couldn't see how to put my life back together, especially with such a huge piece missing. The shock I experienced from my loss came suddenly and knocked at the foundations of my life. I went through the motions, walking disconnected through the next hours and days and months.

Shock is the first stage of grief that takes you into the valley of the shadow of death. Through this experience, I learned that shock has emotional and physical characteristics:

- Feeling numb, disconnected, or emotionally unavailable.
- Feeling as if what you are experiencing is not real.
- Being unable to respond to the daily activities going on around you, almost as though you have tunnel vision. Keeping up with activities and events is a struggle.
- Isolating or avoiding anyone or anything that would require more emotional energy than you have available.
- Having recurring thoughts of the moment you experienced the loss. It becomes marked in your memory— where you were and what you were doing.
- The inability to remember things that happened during the initial shock of loss.
- Withdrawing and seeking comfort from food, drugs, alcohol, or other addictive behaviors.

The way we respond or cope with loss when we are in shock can send us down the path of grieving or get us stuck in shock for years. Even if we know the Lord, our anguish can drive us to find a shortcut to relieve the pain. Our response during this season is vital to our future and well-being.

If you have experienced shock in any form, look back at the physical and emotional characteristics. Make a list of any responses to loss you can identify:

_____

_____

_____

Let's look at the truth of God's Word from Psalm 23:4:

> Yea, though I walk through the valley of the shadow of death, I will fear no evil; for You are with me; Your rod and Your staff, they comfort me. (Psalm 23:4)

This Psalm was my assurance from the Lord that He was with me.

Give an example of a time when you felt God's presence or help in a difficult situation.

_____

_____

_____

_____

Let's apply the truth of God's Word from Psalm 23:4 and declare it today:

- I believe God is with me when I walk through difficult times.
- I will not be fearful even when I am in the darkest valley.
- God's comfort and love surround me and take away my fear.

CHAPTER 2

Anger

As the cloud disappears and vanishes away, so he who goes
down to the grave does not come up. He shall never return to
his house, nor shall his place know him anymore. Therefore,
I will not restrain my mouth; I will speak in the anguish of
my spirit; I will complain in the bitterness of my soul.

—Job 7:9–11

The emotion of anger is often felt when a loss occurs, especially
when it is sudden. Anger signals something is not right with your
situation. If you have prepared for the loss of a loved one, you may
not experience anger, but other members of your family might be
dealing with the stress of family interactions which might elicit
angry responses.

Anger can be expressed as: displeasure, resentment, bitterness, frustration, irritation, indignation, or rage. It is possible to
exhibit any or all of these overwhelming emotions while you are
trying to get your footing on the path of grieving.

Job expressed anguish and bitterness of his soul and spirit as he grieved the loss of his family. The dictionary meaning for *anguish* is "severe mental or physical pain or suffering." Job expressed the grief of his spirit to God.

When we experience the loss of something or someone we expected to always be present in our life, emotions should be expressed. The challenge comes when we get trapped and stay in the place of anger for too long. It is possible to get stuck questioning God while anger and bitterness grow in our heart.

> Be angry and do not sin. Meditate within
> your heart on your bed, and be still. *Selah.*
> Offer the sacrifices of righteousness, and put
> your trust in the LORD. (Psalm 4:4–5)

Ask yourself the following question and write out the answers: What emotions do you still experience because of your loss (anger, displeasure, resentment, bitterness, frustration, irritation, indignation, or rage)?

_____

_____

_____

_____

Who are you holding responsible for your loss?

_____

_____

_____

_____

Most situations are beyond our control. Whenever we experience a loss, we need to recognize this. When we experience that feeling of being out of control, anger, fear, and anxiety often appear—sometimes all at the same time.

Describe any anger, fear, or anxiety you might be feeling.

_____

_____

_____

_____

_____

Take your anger, fear, and anxiety to the Lord. Here are promises from God's Word:

> Therefore, humble yourselves under the mighty hand of God, that He may exalt you in due time, casting all your care upon Him, for He cares for you. (1 Peter 5:6–7)

Be anxious for nothing, but in everything by prayer and supplication, with thanksgiving, let your requests be made known to God; and the peace of God, which surpasses all understanding, will guard your hearts and minds through Christ Jesus. (Philippians 4:6–7)

Make the following declarations:

- I recognize some things still concern me, and I will make them known to God. Like Job, I will write them down and speak them out.
- I cast all my emotions of anger, fear, and anxiety upon you, Lord.
- I will not be anxious, but I will respond to my concerns with prayer and thanksgiving.

A Prayer You Can Pray

Father God, You know the concerns of my heart, and I cast all my cares upon You. I give You every anxious thought, every fear, and every emotion of anger about the loss I have experienced. I give You the person I have held responsible. Thank You for answering my prayer even before I ask it. Father, your Word says when I make my requests known to You,

You will give me a peace beyond my understanding. I thank You for that peace today! In Jesus's name, amen.

CHAPTER 3

Sadness

The pains of death surrounded me, and the pangs of Sheol laid
hold of me; I found trouble and sorrow. Then I called upon the
name of the LORD: "O LORD, I implore You, deliver my soul!"
Gracious is the LORD, and righteous; Yes, our God is merciful.
—Psalm 116:3–5

S adness of heart is like carrying a dark cloud around waiting for
the rain. At any moment, the rain spills from the sky without a hint
of when it will subside. The sadness I felt did not come right away,
but it was another step down the path of grieving. The shock I
experienced left me in a place overwhelmed by what happened the
morning my husband died. I was in a dead zone where emotions
were unavailable to me.

Your friends and family can't always detect your shock from
a loss. Anger can hide deep within you, but sadness is something
that can't hide. God made us to express sadness through our eyes
and tears.

"When Job's friends heard of all the trouble he had gone through, they got together to mourn with him. When they saw him, they could hardly recognize him and were moved with compassion, even weeping for him" (Job 2:11–13). Because of the affliction, Job could not hide his sorrow and grief. His body and face reflected how he felt. His friends were moved with compassion.

> "Now when Job's three friends heard of all this adversity that had come upon him, each one came from his own place—Eliphaz the Temanite, Bildad the Shuhite, and Zophar the Naamathite. For they had made an appointment together to come and mourn with him, and to comfort him. And when they raised their eyes from afar and did not recognize him, they lifted their voices and wept; and each one tore his robe and sprinkled dust on his head toward heaven. So they sat down with him on the ground seven days and seven nights, and no one spoke a word to him, for they saw that his grief was very great" (Job 2:11–13).

Job's friends did four things that Job needed. List those four things:

_____

_____

_____

_____

You may have answered that these men sat silently for seven days and nights with Job. They wept with him, waited till he spoke first, and then listened to hear what he had to say. But Job's friends didn't always have words of comfort. As Job struggled with his thoughts, God showed up to offer full assurance that He was in control of all things. Job's response to God acknowledged this truth: "I know that You can do everything, and that no purpose of Yours can be withheld from You" (Job 42:2).

When we're sad, we need comfort. We need friends who will sit with us, weep with us, and listen to our story. We need a word from the Lord to assure us He has everything in His hands. Sadness is a necessary and normal reaction to loss. Our problem comes when we try to dismiss or avoid the sadness.

Even if you know the Lord, your pain can drive you to find a shortcut to cope with your need for comfort. You can get stuck in cycles trying to meet that need for yourself.

The drive for comfort is at the root of most addictions. Here are some ways most people learn to cope:

- Eating
- Shopping
- Alcohol or drugs (including prescription drugs)
- Isolating and withdrawing
- Sleeping
- Sex

Have you used one or more things mentioned above to comfort yourself? List some ways you have learned to cope:

_____

_____

_____

You may have experienced waves of sadness at unexpected times. Some triggers to sadness include:

- A word
- A sound
- A song
- A memory
- A smell
- A voice.

Look back at the triggers to sadness and identify any you have experienced:

_____

_____

_____

One trigger that took me to sadness was hearing Christmas songs—not the songs about the birth of Jesus, but walking-in-a-winter-wonderland and sitting-by-the-fire type of songs. Several years after my husband's death, I asked some friends to pray for me to release this trigger. This prayer was answered, and I was free to walk through stores without waves of sadness during the Christmas season.

Job's friends were with him as he processed his grief. My encouragement to you is not to do this alone. There is a temptation to isolate when you are hurting, but don't give in to it. You may think no one knows the depth of your loss or how difficult it is for you to see their life continuing when your life has been so severely affected. But you must press through to get to the other side of the sadness. If you isolate, loneliness can take the grieving to another painful level. Seek out your friends, and share your heart even through the tears.

Most importantly, cry out to the Lord. Jesus is the one who heals your heart.

In Luke 4, Jesus read from the Scripture in Isaiah 61 and said, "Today this Scripture is fulfilled in your hearing" (Luke 4:21). God sent Jesus to heal the brokenhearted; to comfort those who mourn; to give beauty for ashes, the oil of joy for mourning, and a garment of praise for the spirit of heaviness. He has promised a great exchange as we focus on Him.

> The Spirit of the Lord GOD is upon Me, because the LORD has anointed Me to preach good tidings to the poor; He has sent Me to heal the brokenhearted, to proclaim liberty to the captives, and the opening of the prison to those who are bound; to proclaim the acceptable year

of the LORD, and the day of vengeance of our God; to comfort all who mourn, to console those who mourn in Zion, to give them beauty for ashes, the oil of joy for mourning, the garment of praise for the spirit of heaviness; that they may be called trees of righteousness, the planting of the LORD, that He may be glorified. (Isaiah 61:1–3)

Before His death, Jesus prepared His disciples—who were troubled by Jesus's words about going away. Jesus said the Holy Spirit would be with the disciples to bring comfort. Followers of Jesus have the same Holy Spirit living inside.

And I will ask the Father, and He will give you another Comforter (Counselor, Helper, Intercessor, Advocate, Strengthener, and Standby), that He may remain with you forever—the Spirit of Truth, whom the world cannot receive (welcome, take to its heart), because it does not see Him or know and recognize Him. But you know and recognize Him, for He lives with you [constantly] and will be in you. (John 14:16–17 AMPC)

Allow the Holy Spirit to bring comfort with the Scriptures. Go through the Psalms, find Scriptures of comfort, and write them down.

Psalm 32:7

_____

_____

_____

_____

Psalm 34:6–7

_____

_____

_____

_____

Psalm 118:5–6

_____

_____

_____

_____

CHAPTER 4

Facing Loss

Nehemiah was a cupbearer for King Artaxerxes. On the day his family—along with some men from Judah—came to visit him, they told Nehemiah the survivors in Jerusalem were in great distress.

> The wall of Jerusalem is also broken down, and its gates are burned with fire. So it was, when I heard these words, that I sat down and wept, and mourned for many days; I was fasting and praying before the God of heaven. (Nehemiah 1:3–4)

During Nehemiah's time of mourning, the king asked him why his countenance was sad. Nehemiah told the king the home of his father lay in waste and asked if he could go to Judah to rebuild. The king gave permission for him to go to Jerusalem to rebuild the walls.

Read Nehemiah 2:11–15. Describe what Nehemiah found when he went out into the night to survey the walls and gates of Jerusalem.

_____

_____

_____

_____

Nehemiah went out by night through the gates of Jerusalem and viewed the walls that were broken down and the gates that were burned with fire. Before Nehemiah could begin the work to rebuild, he needed to survey the damage. After surveying the damage to the walls and gates, he encouraged others to work with him to rebuild. Nehemiah took the time to look at every wall and gate in Jerusalem.

In the same way, it's time for you to survey your land, what you have lost, and how each loss has affected you. Begin by looking at them from a fresh perspective.

You have felt every loss based on your experiences from the past. Any loss that is minimized or ignored will lead to intensified emotions in the next one. The losses you have not grieved will carry weight and add to the weight of the one you are now experiencing.

As you grieve, understand that the wave after wave of shock, anger, and sadness you may experience are all part of the grieving process. The pain you feel is real and must be expressed. As you face the losses in your life, allow yourself to feel the impact of each one, along with every aspect of what that loss means to you.

When my husband died, I lost my friend, my lifestyle, my financial security, my sense of family, hope for my future, a father for my daughter, and a grandfather for my grandchildren. Even though my daughter and I both experienced the loss, I had to recognize that my daughter lost not only her dad but the mom she had known for eleven years, because I was different. I tried my best to keep up with life, but it felt like treading water.

Because my husband and I were joined "as one" in marriage, what remained after his death felt broken like the walls and gates in Jerusalem. Just like Nehemiah, I had to face each missing piece, how I felt about them, and how they affected my life so I could take part in rebuilding what remained.

One way to look at what you have lost is to make a timeline. List the losses you have experienced along the way. Begin with your earliest memory and list them up to age twelve.

This is my loss timeline:

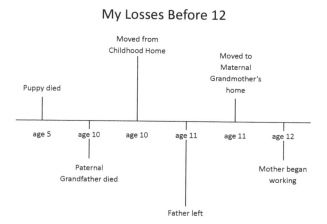

My first loss was a puppy. I was probably around five years old. I remember feeling sad and crying when it happened. When I was ten years old, my paternal grandfather died. We lived next to him and my grandmother. I remember spending more time on my grandfather's lap than my dad's.

My dad was an alcoholic, and his father's death sent him into a downward spiral that he didn't recover from until he lost almost everything. We moved out of the county to another town, so we lost the relationship we had with my paternal grandmother.

Within the next year, my father abandoned our family. We moved in with our maternal grandmother and aunt and attended a new school. My mom now had to find work. For me, the years between the ages of ten and twelve were full of significant loss.

Now it's time to process your losses. List and identify any you experienced during your childhood up to the age of twelve. The ones you experienced in childhood are significant to note because you did not have the tools that adults have to process them. Take the time to write about your memory of each one, how you felt about it when it occurred, and how it affected you.

Make a timeline of your life. Start with your birth, then add years up to the age of twelve. List your losses on the timeline.

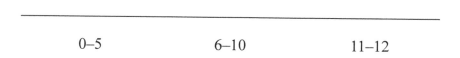

0–5 6–10 11–12

My loss timeline after the age of twelve:

My Losses

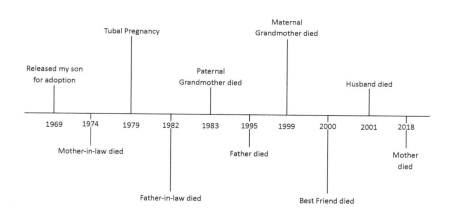

Growing up without a father in my teenage years left me in a vulnerable position where I looked for love in all the wrong places. What I thought was love in a relationship was not love. My inappropriate sexual relationship with a young man resulted in pregnancy as a seventeen-year-old. I spent my eighteenth birthday in a home for unwed mothers and released my child (which was my one and only son) for adoption in 1969.

In 1974, my mother-in-law died suddenly. My husband and I were in our early twenties. We had just finished college and moved away from home to begin our first teaching assignment. My husband was close to his mother, and her death was a significant loss.

In 1979, I experienced a tubal pregnancy, resulting in the loss of another child and the opportunity to be a mother.

In 1982, my father-in-law died of cancer at the age of sixty-two. This was another difficult loss for my husband who had unresolved issues with his dad. My husband had not grieved the death of his mother and was stuck in anger and sadness.

In 1983, my paternal grandmother died. I lost relationship with my grandmother when my father left our family. I didn't go to my grandmother's funeral and never grieved her loss.

In 1995, my father died. I forgave him the year before he died and had a chance to visit with him.

In 1999, my maternal grandmother died in the hospital after falling and breaking her hip. She was ninety-six.

In 2000, my best friend died of cancer.

In 2001, my husband died of cardiac arrest at age fifty-three. The hole in my life left me devastated. I tried to pick up the pieces and put them back together.

In 2018, my mother died at age ninety-one after being homebound from a stroke for seven and a half years, which gave me time to prepare for her death. Because I had already grieved previous losses in my life, the weight of them did not add to this one.

I was free to rejoice as my mother stepped out of this life into heaven.

Now look at your life after the age of twelve and think about the losses you have experienced. Identify them and make a list. Then take the time to write about your memory of each one, how you felt about it, when it occurred, and how it affected you.

_____

_____

_____

_____

_____

_____

_____

_____

Make another timeline beginning with age thirteen to process the losses from your youth to the present time. List them on the timeline.

_____

13   20   30   40   50   60   70

Your timeline is completed by naming each loss and processing how each one has affected you.

Before we proceed further down the grieving path, let's take time to look at ways you attempted to meet your own need to be comforted.

In the Word, there is an example of someone who tried to meet their own needs. God promised an heir to Abram, and that heir would come from his own body. Read Genesis 15:1–4 and Genesis 16:1–3. Sarai planned a way to help God. In Genesis 16:1–3, how did Sarai try to meet that need?

_____

_____

_____

_____

You may have answered that Sarai gave her maid Hagar to be Abram's wife so that she could obtain children through her. It rarely goes well when we try to help God. God's work must be accomplished His way. When we try to replace something or someone with a substitute, we are not facing the loss. When we choose a replacement, we are only delaying the grieving process.

If you haven't dealt with the losses in your life, you might be subject to the schemes of the enemy to redirect God's plan for you. This happened with Sarai and Abram when Sarai made the choice not to wait on God.

Replacing someone you lost with someone else can also cause you to live in fear of losing that person because you did not grieve the loss. Avoid the temptation to help God replace whatever you have lost. We must take our burdens to the Lord and ask for His help through the pain. Psalm 55:22 (NKJV) says, "Cast your burden on the Lord, and He shall sustain you.".

Finish this assignment with the following declarations:

> For I know that my Redeemer lives. (Job 19:25)

> Lord, I give you the burden of my loss and ask you to sustain me. (Psalm 55:22)

> You have kept track of all my wandering and my weeping. You have stored my many tears in your bottle; not one is lost. For they are recorded in your book of remembrance. (Psalm 56:8)

Write a Prayer to the Lord

_____

_____

_____

_____

CHAPTER 5

Forgiveness

For if you forgive men their trespasses, your heavenly Father
will also forgive you. But if you do not forgive men their
trespasses, neither will your Father forgive your trespasses.

—Matthew 6:14–15

After you face any type of loss, the next step down the pathway of grieving is to look at who you hold responsible or blame. As you identify that person, you must go to the next step: forgiveness. Why is it necessary to forgive? Jesus said if you want your Heavenly Father to forgive you, you must forgive others and yourself.

> And whenever you stand praying, if you
> have anything against anyone, forgive him,
> that your Father in heaven may also forgive
> you your trespasses. But if you do not forgive,
> neither will your Father in heaven forgive your
> trespasses. (Mark 11:25–26)

Remember that list you made of people you have held responsible for your loss in chapter 2? It's time to deal with that list. Let's look at a biblical example of how Job's wife responded to Job's loss. She held God responsible for what happened to Job. Her response shows her heart.

> Then his wife said to him, "Do you still hold fast to your integrity? Curse God and die!" But he said to her, "You speak as one of the foolish women speaks. Shall we indeed accept good from God, and shall we not accept adversity?" In all this, Job did not sin with his lips. (Job 2:9–10)

Forgiveness clears the record of wrong that you are holding. The blood of Jesus paid the price for your sin. That same blood paid for the sin of the one you hold responsible for your loss. You must forgive them and move through this step. It is the pivotal point of your grieving process. Do you need more encouragement to forgive?

Read Matthew 18:21. What question did Peter asked Jesus?

_____

_____

_____

Peter asked Jesus how often he should forgive his brother who sinned against him. The answer to the question about forgiveness led to a parable of the unforgiving servant in Matthew 18:22–35. Read the parable and write out the point Jesus made about forgiveness. (You will find the answer in verses 33–35.)

_____

_____

_____

_____

The point Jesus made about forgiveness was that the unforgiving servant should have had compassion on his fellow servant. He should have extended the same pity he received from the master. The master was angry because of his actions and delivered him to the torturers until he paid all that was due. Jesus said His Heavenly Father would do the same to those who do not forgive.

The King James Version of Matthew 18:34 uses the word *tormentors* instead of *torturers*. Would you hang on to unforgiveness if you knew you would experience torment every time you think of the person you hold responsible for your loss? Would you choose the way of unforgiveness if you knew God would not forgive you? Your best choice is to forgive that person you hold responsible for loss.

A Biblical Example of Forgiveness

Read the story of Joseph in Genesis 37–45. Joseph experienced a series of rejections and the loss of his family. But God used these difficult circumstances to send Joseph to Egypt to ultimately save his family and the lives of the children of Israel.

There came a time of famine, and Joseph's family needed help. His brothers left for Egypt to buy some grain because they heard there was grain in Egypt. Little did they know God's plan was for them to meet the brother they had betrayed. God used a time of trouble to bring about a reconciliation between brothers and restore a son to his Father.

The brothers had a lesson to learn about forgiveness. Joseph's destiny was revealed when he met his betrayers and saw his God-given dream fulfilled. Joseph learned not to live out of the pain of his past but to walk into his destiny. Did Joseph blame his brothers for his losses?

Write out Joseph's response to his brothers in Genesis 45:5–8:

_____

_____

_____

_____

Your response may have included several ideas. Joseph told his brothers not to grieve or be angry with themselves because they sold him. He said God had sent him before them to preserve their life. Joseph acknowledged that God made him a ruler throughout the land of Egypt.

My Experience with Forgiveness

One day during a revival meeting at church, I surrendered everything to God and asked Him to take my life and use it. As I poured out my heart to Him and wept, it was as if Jesus tapped me on the shoulder and said, "I forgave you, so now you must forgive." I knew Jesus was saying I needed to forgive my dad. I also wanted the son I released for adoption to forgive me. If I wanted forgiveness, I had to extend it. At that very moment, I made a choice to obey the Lord's instruction.

After this experience, I sent a card to my dad for Father's Day for the first time. I shared in this card how God had stepped into my life to be my Heavenly Father and told him about my adopted daughter. He wrote a letter back to me. It was my first and only letter from him. I visited him during that summer, and our encounter confirmed my forgiveness toward him was complete. Compassion for him welled up inside of me. Exactly one year later, my father died. I experienced the peace of the Lord, knowing I had set things right in our relationship.

You will find as you forgive the one you are holding responsible for the losses in your life, you will receive the peace of the Lord that passes all understanding.

A Prayer You Can Pray

Father, there is still pain when I think about what I have lost. I have held _____ responsible for the loss of _____. Today I choose to forgive _____ and no longer hold him/her responsible. Father, wash me clean of unforgiveness held in my heart. I ask You to remove the pain and bring healing to my heart. In Jesus's name, amen.

CHAPTER 6

Release

Peace, I leave with you, My peace I give to you;
not as the world gives, do I give to you. Let not
your heart be troubled, neither let it be afraid.

—John 14: 27

T he next step down the grieving path is to release the one you hold responsible for the loss you have experienced. *Release* means to set free. It also means you no longer hold them accountable. Jesus took forgiveness to this level when He said, "Father, forgive them, for they do not know what they do" (Luke 23:34). He gave us a clear picture in Matthew of what forgiveness looks like: "But I say to you, love your enemies, bless those who curse you, do good to those who hate you, and pray for those who spitefully use you and persecute you" (Matthew 5:44).

List the four things Jesus instructed you to do for those who hurt you:

1. _____

2. _____

3. _____

4. _____

Jesus said, (1) love your enemies, (2) bless those who curse you, (3) do good to those who hate you, (4) and pray for those who spitefully use you and persecute you.

Follow these instructions by Jesus, and you will receive the peace He offers in John 14. After you have released the person you held responsible, you are able to release what you lost. "Peace, I leave with you, My peace I give to you; not as the world gives, do I give to you. Let not your heart be troubled, neither let it be afraid" (John 14:27).

Naomi's Story

In the book of Ruth, we find the story of Naomi and how she released what she lost and began to look forward to her future. Naomi lost her home and husband's inheritance in Bethlehem when she followed her husband to Moab because there was a famine in Judah. While in Moab, Naomi lost her husband and two sons, leaving her with two daughters-in-law in a foreign country.

Naomi's losses were great, and she had to face them. After hearing God was providing food for His people, she made a decision to return to the land of Judah. Her plan was to release what she had lost in her husband and sons and what was still in her life: her two daughters-in-law.

Read Ruth 1:8–9. What was Naomi's plan for her daughters-in-law?

_____

_____

_____

_____

Naomi's plan was to send her daughters-in-law back to their family to marry again.

Ruth told Naomi she would follow her to Judah. Ruth was ready to release the loss of her own husband, but she was not going to release what God had given her: a mother-in-law.

> Then they lifted up their voices and wept again; and Orpah kissed her mother-in-law; but Ruth clung to her, and she said,
> "Look, your sister-in-law has gone back to her people and to her gods; return after your sister-in-law" (Ruth 1:14–15).

Read Ruth 1:16–18 What was Ruth's plan for her future?

_____

_____

_____

_____

Ruth pleaded with Naomi not to ask her to leave her. She declared that she would go wherever Naomi would go. Ruth said Naomi's people would be her people, and Naomi's God would be her God.

When Naomi returned to Bethlehem, she was still bitter over her losses. She thought God afflicted her with what she experienced. She could only see what had been taken away, leaving little hope for a future in Moab or her husband's ancestral home. Thank God Naomi did not remain hopeless and bitter.

Naomi was a widow who submitted to God's _now_ plan. She followed the leading from God to return to the home of her husband's people. She allowed Ruth to find a field in which to glean heads of grain so they would have food. I believe that each day, Naomi's hope was growing in what God would do with her situation. She recognized God's provision of a next of kin who had the right of redemption of her husband's ancestral land.

If Naomi stayed in a place of bitterness, she would not have received the blessing that came through Ruth and Boaz and their child, Obed. The joy of bouncing her grandchild on her knees was redemption for losing her husband and sons. The joy of the hope of the future replaced her mourning. Now we can see from this side of "His-story," the ancestral line of King David and the Messiah, Jesus, coming through Naomi, Ruth, Boaz, and Obed—their son.

Declare today:

- I release the one I have held responsible for my loss.
- I will love, bless, do something good, and pray for the person I released.
- I release what I have lost, and I accept how God will use this in my life.
- I receive the peace offered by Jesus that only He can give.

A Prayer You Can Pray

Father, today I release the hurt and pain I have held in my heart. I release _____ (the person you have held responsible) whom I have held captive in my heart, expecting them to pay for what I have lost. I release the loss that was in my past and my plans for my future to you, Lord. In Jesus's name, amen.

CHAPTER 7

Facing the Reality of the Loss

I would have lost heart, unless I had believed that I would
see the goodness of the LORD in the land of the living.

—Psalm 27:13

The healing process of your heart begins when you step out of
the shock of what happened that changed your life, release your
emotions of anger and sadness, and face what or whom you've
lost. Restoration of your heart continues as you look at how you
are coping with those losses, forgiving those you blame, and
releasing them to the Father.

The next step on the healing path is facing reality. This step
requires daily walking out how your life has changed and dealing
with the reminders of the loss. As you face these realities, you
may experience sadness again. You will need to forgive, release
your loss, and step into your new reality to continue through your
healing process.

As I faced the daily reality of being without my husband, I
had many opportunities to cry out to the Lord for His help. He

gave me direction through dreams, promises in His Word, and a series of open and shut doors.

God filled my loss of a life partner with His presence. Right after Jack's death, as the waves of grief came, I held on to the promises of God. One promise was in Isaiah 26:3: "You will keep him in perfect peace, whose mind is stayed on You, because he trusts in You."

I found that perfect peace comes with praising God and calling out to Him. This kind of peace was what I prayed for, and it came as I felt the presence of the Holy Spirit. God's provision of perfect peace also came through, knowing Jack had accepted Jesus as his Savior and Lord. I was sure that as we laid Jack's earthly body to rest, his heavenly body was joining the angels in praising God.

During the early months of my loss, God provided several opportunities to go on retreat so I could focus on Him. In one retreat at The Cove in Black Mountain, North Carolina, a scripture hung on the wall in my room. God burned that Scripture on my heart. "Trust in the Lord with all your heart and lean not on your own understanding, In all your ways, acknowledge Him, and He shall direct your paths" (Proverbs 3:5–6).

I thanked God for strength to walk through each day as I stood on this promise: "God is our refuge and strength, a very present help in trouble" (Psalm 46:1).

I also thanked God for the gift of my daughter, Molly, and I asked for His help in raising her in the fear and admonition of the Lord. Comfort came in another promise in God's Word: "A father of the fatherless, a defender of widows, is God in His holy habitation" (Psalm 68:5).

As I received God's promises with a thankful heart, He provided direction and answers to my questions. They came in a series of confirmations during a time of great shaking for me and for our nation. One of my prayers was for God to give me a clear vision of His plan for Molly and me. I questioned if I should continue to stay in my home, job, and location.

On the night of September 11, 2001, God gave me the vision of His plan for my life: to leave Smyrna, Georgia, where I had lived with my husband and go back to my hometown in North Carolina to minister to my family and accept their support for me and my daughter. My mother, stepfather, and three of my four sisters lived in North Carolina at that time.

God put things together to make the move possible. For example, when God told me about the move, I knew this was not what Molly would want. I asked God to give her the same vision He gave me.

I watched and waited for God to work in Molly's life. At the end of February 2002, I told her we were going to move to North Carolina. I told Molly all the reasons God had given me for moving. We were to trust Him in all things by submitting to Him. Obeying God without knowing the outcome meant we had to concentrate on what was eternally important instead of what was comfortable and familiar.

Moving would provide an extended family and godly male role models for my daughter. A slower pace of life would enable us to enjoy Molly's last years at home and my mother's last years with us. Since North Carolina was my childhood home, we could explore the woods, mountains, and pastures God had provided for me as a child.

Molly listened to all my reasons for moving. Even as her tears flowed, God did a mighty work. That night at bedtime, before we prayed, Molly said, "Mama, I think God is changing my heart to make me want to go to North Carolina."

I thanked God for answering my prayer. He orchestrated every detail of the move and our life in a new location. My new reality would include a move from the home my husband and I had shared for fifteen years and the only home my daughter had ever known.

We transitioned to our new home in July 2002, a year and six months after my husband died. Those were the most difficult months of my life, and now I was a single mom raising a twelve-year-old daughter in a totally new environment.

I felt the move was important not only for me but for my daughter to develop relationships with my family. Molly moved from a private school in Atlanta to a public school in North Carolina and began seventh grade in the fall. The transition to public school did not go well. By the end of October, I quit my job and began homeschooling.

God provided a wonderful church with a community of moms who were already homeschooling. I had much to learn, but I felt God directing me to just the right community of believers. In this church, Molly and I developed new friendships with believers who loved Jesus. They also loved us and accepted us with open arms.

Yet my daughter and I were two hurting people hurting each other. I knew I needed to break the cycle, but I didn't know how to do it. As I prayed daily for our relationship, I recognized the need for counseling to help us get through our pain, but I didn't know where to go for help.

God provided help through Living Waters Ministry. I read about a retreat in Moravian Falls called "Healing at the Root" in a local Christian newspaper. Denise and Lee Boggs of Living Waters Ministry led the retreat.

I arrived at the retreat in May 2003, not knowing what to expect. I needed healing at the root deep down in my heart. After a time of greeting and gathering for dinner at Apple Hill Lodge, we went downstairs to a room where a garden was created which included a beautiful blue waterfall of draped fabric.

That night, Denise Boggs shared her story of how God brought healing to her heart. As I listened to her story, hope rose in me that God could bring healing to my heart and restore my relationship with my daughter.

Denise talked about how the painful events in her life led to a stony heart that blocked the flow of God's love. I could see where hurts in my past had made a ring of stones around my own heart that protected me and prevented me from feeling pain. These stones also blocked God's love that needed to flow through me to my daughter.

My first step to healing was to recognize the problem. When my father left our family, I was ten years old with pain I didn't know how to process. My family was also hurting, and we lived in a state of dysfunction because of my father's alcoholism. One way we learned to cope with pain was not to talk about it. That response gave no place to process the feelings of rejection and abandonment. I justified my sinful reactions of anger, bitterness, and rebellion toward my father because of his actions.

Even though ten years earlier I had a touch from the Lord that brought forgiveness into my heart for my father, I still wrestled with issues of rejection and abandonment—which I did not realize were still there. My daughter was also experiencing the same issues because of her adoption and her father's death. Her rejection issues touched my rejection issues, and a great stone wall of hurt kept us from sharing our heart and love for each other. In order for me to help Molly heal, I needed to heal first.

Part of that healing was a time of writing letters to my mother and father to express how I felt when the events of my childhood occurred. These letters were a way of expressing the pain still in my heart. I didn't give the letters to my mom, and my father had already passed. But writing the letters helped me recognize what happened that caused the pain in my heart and my sinful reactions.

I repented to the Lord for the anger, resentment, and rebellion that came into my heart during this time. I asked the Lord to forgive me for my sinful responses to my parents.

This retreat began a path of healing for me and my daughter which has continued through many setbacks and trials. Through the years, God has brought healing in our relationship and restoration in my life that I never imagined could be possible.

A Biblical Example of Facing the Reality of a Loss

Let's continue with Naomi and Ruth's story from the last chapter. Ruth faced the reality of the loss of a provider for herself and Naomi. She recognized the daily need for food to sustain them. The need for provision and Ruth's willingness to step into the reality of that need for food brought about a divine appointment. Ruth was looking for favor (Ruth 2:2), and she found it when Boaz noticed her.

Read Ruth 2:10–12. What reason did Boaz give for his favor and blessing over Ruth that God would reward her?

_____

_____

_____

_____

Your response may have included the following ideas: Boaz heard what Ruth had done for her mother-in-law since the death of her husband and how she had left the land of her birth to come with Naomi to Bethlehem.

Ruth stepped out into the field to glean heads of wheat and found favor in the eyes of the owner of the field. Her willingness to embrace Naomi, follow her back to her homeland, and embrace her people brought a blessing and a reward.

Naomi recognized the hand of God that could redeem her situation. Naomi sent Ruth on a mission recorded in Ruth 3:3–4. Read this scripture and describe what Naomi sent Ruth to do.

_____

_____

_____

_____

You may have answered that Naomi told Ruth to wash and anoint herself, put on her best garment, and go down to the threshing floor. She should not make herself known until Boaz had finished eating and drinking. Then when he laid down to sleep, she should go in, uncover his feet, lie down, and listen to what he would tell her to do.

Naomi and Boaz both knew about the right to redeem property (Leviticus 25:23–28) and the duty of a husband's brother to preserve the family line in Israel (Deuteronomy 25:5). However, Boaz knew he was not the closest relative to Naomi. Read Ruth 3:12–13 and record what Boaz promised Ruth.

_____

_____

_____

_____

Boaz said if the relative closest to Naomi would not perform the duty to preserve the family line, he would do it. He went up to the city gate and spoke to Naomi's closest relative.

After communicating the plight of Naomi and the right he had to buy back and redeem the land, his first response was that he would redeem it. But after Boaz spoke that this right included Ruth, he had an entirely different response. Read Ruth 4:6 and record his response.

_____

_____

_____

_____

The close relative said he could not buy back the field because it would ruin his own inheritance. He told Boaz he could redeem the right of redemption.

Read Ruth 4:9–10 and record two things Boaz claimed as his right to redeem.

1. _____

2. _____

Boaz claimed he bought all that belonged to Naomi's husband from Naomi, and he acquired Ruth as his wife to perpetuate the name and family line through his inheritance.

As Ruth and Naomi faced their loss, they began to walk into the new reality of their life. God stepped in and initiated a process of redemption. Ruth asked for favor, and God answered. Naomi recognized the opportunity of a blessing from God and asked Ruth to step into it. God provided the opportunity and the redeemer.

God's way is to *redeem* (buy back, ransom) what we've lost. Sometimes our way is to *replace* what we've lost. Respond to the following question:

1. Have I faced the reality of the loss, or have I replaced it with:

   • a physical object
   • a pet
   • a person
   • a habit or activity

   _____

   _____

   _____

   _____

2. How have I stepped out into the reality of the loss?

   _____

   _____

   _____

   _____

3. What have I seen God redeem in my loss?

_____

_____

_____

_____

4. What challenges am I facing?

_____

_____

_____

_____

5. What opportunities do I see in my situation?

_____

_____

_____

_____

Now may the God of hope fill you with all joy and peace in believing, that you may abound in hope by the power of the Holy Spirit. (Romans 15:13)

A Prayer You Can Pray

Father, today I ask for Your joy and peace to flood me as I trust in You. Overflow me with Your hope today by the power of the Holy Spirit. In Jesus's name, amen.

Chapter 8

Final Release

Sing praise to the Lord, you saints of His, and give
thanks at the remembrance of His holy name. For His
anger is but for a moment, His favor is for life; weeping
may endure for a night, but joy comes in the morning.

—Psalm 30:4–5

On this path, you descended into the valley of the shadow of
death. Now you will soar higher as you ascend the last steps of
grieving your loss. It's time for you to release the life you have
been holding on to, your expectations, and disappointments.

Surrendering your way to the Lord makes room for God's
way in your life. You may find that you have been holding on to
things you used to replace what you lost. Release them too. As you
release, your hands will be open to receive.

For me, the final release of what I lost looked like the surrender of my will and my ways and acceptance of God's will and His
ways. The scripture I wrote in my journal the day before my husband's death was Psalm 18:30. I look back on that scripture as a

message to reassure me that God had me in His hands and I could trust Him. "As for God, His way is perfect. The word of the LORD is proven; He is a shield to all who trust in Him" (Psalm 18:30).

A Biblical Example of Final Release

In the book of Mark, Jesus spoke to the disciples about all He would suffer, His death, and His resurrection.

Read Mark 8:31–34. Write Peter's response to Jesus in Mark 8:32.

_____

_____

_____

_____

Peter took Jesus aside and began to rebuke Him.

What did Jesus say when He rebuked Peter in Mark 8:33?

_____

_____

_____

_____

You could have answered that Jesus told Peter he was not thinking about the things of God. He was thinking from man's perspective.

Jesus told the disciples they would need to do three things in Mark 8:34. List them below.

1. _____

2. _____

3. _____

Jesus told the disciples they would need to:

- deny themselves
- take up His cross
- follow Him

In the book *Absolute Surrender*, Andrew Murray wrote about Peter's response to Jesus in Mark 8:33. He says Peter had to learn a lesson before the Lord could use him mightily through the power of the Holy Spirit. He had to surrender his self-will, his flesh. Jesus said, "...deny yourself..." (Mark 8:34). The admonition Christ gave to Peter was part of his training. Peter's failure came when he did not surrender to God's way. Andrew Murray said when Peter did not deny himself, he later denied Jesus.

My Experience with Final Release

When Jack died, I felt the crushing weight of responsibility of raising Molly by myself. When my father left us, my mother became a single mom of five children. I watched how it affected her and how she worked and focused on providing for our family. She didn't have the time to see what was happening to me as I negotiated feelings of rejection and abandonment.

Our family didn't talk about how we felt about the things that came up daily at school with our friends. I was not prepared to deal with dating and the emotions that drove me to seek attention and affection from a relationship. I was not prepared for the consequences of my choices that led me to getting pregnant and giving up my son for adoption.

As my daughter moved into her teenage years, I did not want her to repeat the choices I made as a teen. I felt I needed to protect her from anyone who would take advantage of her. I projected my poor decisions on her and feared she would make the same choices because she was also growing up without a father.

I thought if I could get involved in Molly's youth group and get to know her friends, I could protect her. I was like a guard in a basketball game protecting the ball. I know now that I was operating out of the fear of losing her. What looked like protection to me looked like control to my daughter. The more I controlled her, the more she wanted to get away from me.

Releasing my daughter to fulfill her God-given destiny did not come easily for me. After eighteen years of nurturing, encouraging, protecting, and teaching, there came a time for me to retreat and allow my daughter to step out on the path God had planned for her. I had to release *my* plan and allow God to direct my daughter toward *His* plan. But I can assure you God had to do a work in me to pry my fingers off the control button. I believe as I released Molly to the Lord, it freed her to hear from Him.

Are you ready to receive the divine exchange: beauty for ashes, oil of joy for mourning, the garment of praise for the spirit of heaviness (Isaiah 61:3)? Now is the time to raise your hopes and expectations for what God has in store for you.

A Prayer You Can Pray

Father God, today I thank You for Your Word that says weeping may endure for a night, but joy comes in the morning. Thank you that Your Word says You will strengthen and help me. Thank you for holding me with Your righteous right hand.

Father, today I release the things I have been holding on to, and I receive Your plans for me. I release my worry and anxious thoughts to You. I release my will and ask that Your will be done in my life. I also release what I have used to replace what I lost. I am ready to receive the divine exchange of beauty for ashes, the oil of joy for mourning, and the garment of praise for the spirit of heaviness. Thank you, Father. In Jesus's name, amen.

CHAPTER 9

Acceptance

You have turned for me my mourning into dancing; you
have put off my sackcloth and clothed me with gladness,
to the end that my glory may sing praise to You and not be
silent. O LORD my God, I will give thanks to You forever.
—Psalm 30:11–12

On this last step of your grieving path, it's time to change your
perspective. This step opens the door to accept and receive an
exchange. You are ready to embrace your new life with changes
that redeem your losses.

God's way is to exchange our grieving for gladness and
joy. It's time to see God do what only He can do. You have been
through a significant battle. You have cried out to the Lord, and He
has answered. He has strengthened you and given you the keys to
His plan for your life in this season.

Esther

Let's look for a moment at a biblical example of someone who accepted and embraced the assignment on her life after loss.

In the book of Esther, we find a young Jewish woman. She lost both her mother and father, so a close relative named Mordecai raised her. King Ahasuerus planned to replace Queen Vashti with a new queen. Esther was one of the young maids chosen to begin beauty preparations to ready her for an appearance before the king. Mordecai instructed Esther not to reveal her Jewish heritage.

Esther accepted her assignment. She was taken to the custodian of the women and found *favor* with him (Esther 2:9). Does this remind you of Ruth who found *favor* with Boaz? Watch for this word to come up again in Esther's story.

Read Esther 2:12. Describe Esther's beauty preparations below:

_____

_____

_____

_____

Esther's beauty preparations were completed over twelve months. There were six months with oil of myrrh and six months with perfumes and preparations for beautifying women.

Read Esther 2:15–17 and find two times Esther found favor.

1. _____

2. _____

Esther found favor with all who saw her. She received grace and favor in the king's sight more than all the other young women. The crown Esther accepted came with a challenge. She could have thought her challenge was getting beautiful for the king or being chosen as one among many to be queen. But her challenge had just begun. The real battle was to save her Jewish people from annihilation.

One day, Mordecai revealed a plot to overthrow the king to Queen Esther, who then informed the king. After the plot was discovered, Haman was promoted to a high position. He was the one she would face in battle. All the king's servants were commanded to bow and pay homage to Haman, but Mordecai refused to bow before him.

Read Esther 3:6 to find what Haman planned for Mordecai and the Jewish people. What was his plan?

_____

_____

_____

_____

Haman's plan was to destroy all the Jews who were through-out the whole kingdom of Ahasuerus—the people of Mordecai.

Mordecai appeared at the king's gate in sackcloth and ashes with a message for Esther. He shared the plan Haman had for the Jewish people and asked her to go to the king and plead for them. Esther knew if she acted on his request, the king could put her to death. Mordecai challenged Esther to accept the new assignment. Read Esther 4:13–14 and record what Mordecai said to Esther.

_____

_____

_____

_____

Mordecai told Esther not to think she would escape the king's palace any more than the other Jews. If she remained silent, relief and deliverance would arise for the Jews from another place, but her father's house would perish. *Who knows whether you have come to the kingdom for such a time as this?*

Her plan was to fast for three days and nights. Esther accepted the challenge and the assignment. "And so, I will go to the king, which is against the law; and if I perish, I perish!" (Esther 4:16). The battles continued with many opportunities for Esther to turn and run or accept God's call on her life. Her story began with the loss of two parents and ended with the redemption of the Jewish people.

My Experience with Accepting God's Plan for Redemption after Loss

As a teenager, my desire for affection and attention led me to look for love in all the wrong places. I chose a shortcut because I wasn't willing to wait for God's plan. That shortcut put me on a path that led to a teen pregnancy and giving up my right to mother my son.

I struggled with my decision and the desire to be a mother for twenty years before God blessed Jack and me with the opportunity to adopt a precious baby girl. I knew the gift He gave was worth the wait. In fact, God used the desire for a child to draw me back to Him. My journey with the Lord began with my daughter's adoption. I received a gift from the Lord that took His daily, moment-by-moment help to steward.

Ten years after Jack's death—forty-two years after I relinquished my right to be a mother to my son—I heard the voice of my son for the first time. The return of my son to my life was above and beyond anything I hoped or imagined God would do for me. Since that moment, I have cherished the gift of redemption from a mistake in my past.

> Instead of your shame you shall have double honor. And instead of confusion they shall rejoice in their portion. Therefore in their land they shall possess double; everlasting joy shall be theirs. (Isaiah 61:7)

Almost twenty-five years ago, the Lord used this scripture from Isaiah to encourage me with His plan to redeem things from my past. I have marveled as the Lord removed shame, covered me with His righteousness, and revealed a double portion.

After the Lord restored the relationship with my son, I'm humbled to say I am blessed with two children and five grandchildren. And my son is a father of twin sons. The Lord has restored double. I am experiencing His everlasting joy!

My encouragement to you is to know that God has restoration in His plans for you, and there is nothing He can't do.

Meditate on the following scriptures:

> You will show me the path of life; in Your presence is fullness of joy; at Your right hand are pleasures forevermore. (Psalm 16:11)

> But let all those rejoice who put their trust in You; let them ever shout for joy, because You defend them; let those also who love Your name be joyful in You. (Psalm 5:11)

> I will greatly rejoice in the Lord, my soul shall be joyful in my God; for He has clothed me with the garments of salvation, He has covered me with the robe of righteousness, as a bridegroom decks himself with ornaments,

and as a bride adorns herself with her jewels.
(Isaiah 61:10)

A Prayer You Can Pray

Father God, thank You for turning my mourning into dancing. Thank You for the great exchange of my sorrow for joy. Father, I will rejoice in the redemption that You have planned in my life even before I see it. Every day I will seek Your presence and Your path for my life. In Jesus's name I pray, amen.

CHAPTER 10

Overcomers

The LORD is my shepherd; I shall not want. He makes
me to lie down in green pastures. He leads me beside
the still waters. He restores my soul. He leads me in
the paths of righteousness for His name's sake.

—Psalm 23:1–3

David knew God's restoring power was available to him. God
provided David with places to rest (green pastures and still waters),
direction of how to rest (to lie down), the reward for resting (God
restored David's soul when he rested in His love), and then He led
David in the paths of righteousness. With God's help and direction, David became an overcomer. Study the chart below to see
what David overcame.

David overcame:	Scripture:
a lion, a bear, and Goliath	1 Samuel 17:31–51
rejection	1 Samuel 17:28
depression	Psalm 42:5
betrayal	2 Samuel 15:1–6

disappointment	1 Chronicles 17:1–4
adultery and murder through repentance	Psalm 51:1–4
loss	2 Samuel 12:16–23

There was a restoration promise in Psalm 23 for David. God restored his soul. God's promise for those who overcome is the reward of restoration. Let's look at each person mentioned in this Bible study and what they overcame. Write what God restored to their life in the chart below.

Name/Loss	Scripture	Restored
Job overcame loss	Job 42:10	
Naomi overcame loss and bitterness	Ruth 4:14–15	
Joseph overcame rejection, abandonment, accusation, prison, and famine	Genesis 45:3–8	
Esther overcame loss, fear of death, and fear of the king	Esther 9:20–22	
Nehemiah overcame opposition, fatigue, frustration, and fear	Nehemiah 7:1	
Peter overcame his betrayal of Jesus	John 21:15	

You may have answered this way: God restored to Job twice as much as he had before. Naomi received restored hope for her future. Joseph's family was restored to him. Esther's people were restored to favor with the king. Nehemiah was used by God to restore the walls and gates of Jerusalem. Peter's relationship with Jesus was restored.

> And they overcame him by the blood of
> the Lamb and by the word of their testimony,
> and they did not love their lives to the death.
> (Revelation 12:11)

In Revelation 12, Jesus spoke of the way to overcome: the price for redemption that Jesus paid (blood of the Lamb) and the testimony of the saints who surrender their life to Jesus. God made a way for us to overcome. Our part is to share with others how we overcame trials in our life by surrendering them to Jesus.

In this Bible study, you identified things you are overcoming. You received understanding about the grieving process, and you received comfort from the Lord. In this lesson, you have seen God's promised restoration as you continue walking out the grieving path as an overcomer. Now I challenge you to continue down the path of righteousness and embrace what God has for you in the future. I encourage you to share what God has done in your life with others.

> Blessed be the God and Father of our Lord
> Jesus Christ, the Father of mercies and God of
> all comfort, who comforts us in all our tribu-

lation, that we may be able to comfort those who are in any trouble, with the comfort with which we ourselves are comforted by God. (2 Corinthians 1:3–4)

Write your testimony of how God brought healing and restoration to you as you have walked down the grieving path presented in this study. Share this testimony with others. As you share your testimony of what God did for you, God will use you to bring encouragement and support to those walking down their own grieving path. You will be part of God's plan of healing and restoration for others as He restores your soul.

The LORD will guide you continually, and satisfy your soul in drought, and strengthen your bones; you shall be like a watered garden, and like a spring of water, whose waters do not fail. Those from among you shall build the old waste places; you shall raise up the foundations of many generations; and you shall be called the Repairer of the Breach. The Restorer of Streets to Dwell In. (Isaiah 58:11–12)

Your testimony:

About the Author

Ann Rita Frazier is a retired teacher and librarian. She is a mother of two children, five grandchildren, and one great-grandson. Over thirty years ago, she chose to live a life with God's influence and direction. Her path to healing began with grieving the loss of her husband after a thirty-one-year marriage. To contact or read more about the author go to: http://www.annritafrazier.com

CPSIA information can be obtained
at www.ICGtesting.com
Printed in the USA
LVHW032118100322
712917LV00005B/576